Small Business Survival Guide

Small Business Survival Guide

How to Save Money and Thrive During Challenging Times

Josevie F. Jackson

Published by Tablo

Table of Contents

It May Be Hard, But Don't Give Up

Running a small business isn't easy, even during the best of times. According the United States Small Business Association:

- 30% of small businesses fail within two years
- 50% fail within five years
- Only 25% of businesses last 15 years or longer

Any small business owner will tell you that running a small business is challenging. You have to manage a thousand moving pieces, ensuring that you stay on top of cash flow, employee performance, sales, marketing, and many other factors. Many owners struggle to manage all the different elements, and their business struggles as a result.

When circumstances get tough, running a business becomes an even greater challenge. Throughout the years, many events have occurred that placed a squeeze on businesses:

- The Great Depression
- World War I and World War II
- The Cold War
- The 2008 housing market collapse
- The 2020 Coronavirus pandemic

During these difficult times, many small businesses folded under the pressure. They simply weren't able to keep going.

But many businesses have survived these incredibly challenging circumstances. Some of them have even thrived. In the early 1920s, Prohibition prevented the sale of alcohol in the United States. As you can imagine, this made things really difficult for producers of alcohol. In recent times, the Coronavirus caused mandated shutdowns which caused companies to become more resourceful and adjust to changing times.

Many companies adapted and came up with creative ways to save their businesses:

- T3 Expo converted trade show space into a hospital
- ExxonMobile produced hand sanitizer
- Brook Brothers made surgical gowns and masks

The point is that your business can make it through hard times. You just need to get creative. You have to take decisive action. You'll need to make tough decisions. But you can do it!

"Most great people have attained their greatest success just one step beyond their greatest failure."

- NAPOLEON HILL

In his book *How The Mighty Fall*, Jim Collins wrote:

The signature of the truly great versus the merely successful is not the absence of difficulty, but the ability to come back from setbacks, even cataclysmic catastrophes, stronger than before. Great nations can decline and recover. Great companies can fall and recover. Great social institutions can fall and recover. And great individuals can fall and recover. As long as you never get entirely knocked out of the game, there remains always hope.

Don't give up. There is always hope!

In this small business survival guide, you'll discover effective steps to take that will help your business thrive in the midst of difficult times. Doing these things won't make things "easier", but they could be the difference between your business surviving or dying.

Ready? Let's dive in.

Manage Your Mindset

If your business is struggling, it's absolutely essential to manage your mindset. When things get tough, it's really easy to enter a downward mental spiral.

You start thinking about all the circumstances that brought you to where you are. You second guess yourself, wondering whether you would be in a better place if you acted differently. You begin to doubt your abilities and whether you can ever succeed. The more you engage in these thoughts, the worse you'll feel.

As you work to stabilize and turn around your business, it's important to maintain a positive mindset. Now, to be clear, this doesn't mean that you pretend everything is okay or bury your head in the sand. It means that you maintain faith in your ability to bring about positive outcomes.

A positive mindset also means that you are resolved to not give up. Keep striving to improve things and bring your business to a place of health.

If you're struggling to maintain a positive mindset, remember that almost every great business leader has endured struggles similar to yours:

- Thomas Edison failed thousands of times before he was able to develop a fully functioning lightbulb.
- Apple almost collapsed under bankruptcy when Steve Jobs was president.
- Bill Gates' first business was a complete and total failure.
- Henry Ford's first automobile business went bankrupt within a year.

In spite of all these difficulties, these individuals experienced great success. Why? Because they persevered and were incredibly resilient.

Steve Jobs said:

I'm convinced that about half of what separates the successful entrepreneurs from the non-successful ones is pure perseverance. It is so hard and you pour so much of your life into this thing, there are such rough moments in time that most people give up. And I don't blame them, it's really tough.

If you want your business to succeed, you need mental toughness. You must be able to persevere in the face of difficulty and keep going even when things look bleak.

Follow these steps to overcome a negative mindset:

1. Pay attention. It's easy to let negative thoughts swirl in your mind without putting up a fight. If you're going to overcome these thoughts, you must be aware of what

you're thinking. You need to be able to identify unhelpful mental patterns as they occur.

2. Question. As negative thoughts arise, question them. Is what you're thinking really true? Most likely, it isn't. Mentally push back.

3. Silence. After you've questioned and answered your negative thoughts, begin to silence them. Avoid letting the same thoughts steal your mental energy. You know they're not true, so shut them down at the start. Imagine that you have a remote and that you can mute your inner critic with the touch of a button.

4. Replace. As you shut down your inner critic, fill the silence with positive, helpful dialogue. Regularly remind yourself that you are strong, are able to overcome challenges, and are growing in the midst of difficulty.

These steps can also be found in greater detail in my book, *Thrive & Be Somebody, 11 Steps to Maneuver Life's Obstacles with Confidence*. Remember, as you push through problems and challenges, why you got into business in the first place.

What big problem were you passionate about solving? What motivated you to take the risk of starting a business instead of playing it safe and taking a corporate job?

Seek to tap into the emotions and desires that originally pushed you to create your business. They can be the driving force that helps you make tough decisions and get things back on track.

"Some people dream of success, while other people get up every morning and make it happen."- WAYNE HUIZENGA

Before you can identify a solution, it's important to first clarify the problem. Why is your business struggling in the first place? If you don't have clarity on the specific challenge you're facing, you won't know what steps to take to save your business.

Take some time to think about how you got to where you currently are. What happened that you didn't anticipate? What things went wrong?

Some common problems businesses face are:

1. Market changes. Economic factors, new technology, emerging competition, and many other things can cause the market to change. Survival requires the ability to adapt to changes as they happen.

2. Failure to understand the target customer or market. If people aren't interested in your product or service, there's a good chance you don't understand your customers or market. Dig deep to understand what people truly want and what motivates them to buy.

3. Poor pricing strategy. If your prices don't match the customer demand, you simply won't sell much. It's crucial to understand what customers are willing to pay, as well as where your product sits in relation to your competitors.

4. Insufficient funds. Not having enough money on hand will quickly tank your business. You must pay close attention to cash flow, financing, sales, and more.

5. Too much growth. Growth is a good thing except when there's too much of it. If your business grows too fast, you might not be able to keep up with demand.

Identifying key problems within your business can be a painful exercise. No one likes to be reminded of ways they've failed. But if you want your business to thrive during challenging times, you must be able to put your finger on the primary problems.

If you're feeling sick and go to the doctor, what's the first thing they try to do? Determine what is causing the illness.

Only then can the doctor prescribe the proper treatment. If the doctor has you start taking random medications in the hope that one will work, you likely won't get any better.

The same principle is true in business. You must identify the cause of the problems before you can determine the proper solution. The sooner you identify the problems, the better.

As Jim Collins wrote in *Too Mighty To Fall:*

I've come to see institutional decline like a staged disease: harder to detect but easier to cure in the early stages, easier to detect but harder to cure in the later stages. An institution can look strong on the outside but already be sick on the inside...

Focus on Your Customers

Before we get into details about specific actions to take, let's look at the big picture.

What is at the heart of every business, including yours? Customers.

If you don't have customers, you don't have a business. When deciding what actions to take to strengthen your business, always keep your customers front and center. If you make changes that end up hurting your customers, you're ultimately hurting yourself. You'll lose the people who are at the very center of your business.

Airlines are an example of what happens when you forget about your customers. Over the last decade, airlines have gone to great lengths to cut costs and increase profits. Service declined and customers were hit with various fees they never had to pay in the past.

The result? Customers are getting increasingly frustrated and fed up. It seems that everyone has an airline horror story. Flying, which was once seen as a luxury, is now often considered a necessary evil.

The moral of the story is to always keep your customers at the top of the priority list.

Before making changes, consider how they will affect the customer experience. If customer experience is one of your key competitive advantages, be especially careful about changes. If you destroy one of your competitive advantages, you may end up dealing a death blow to your business.

If you do make changes that will directly affect the customer, communicate those clearly. Explain to the customer why you have to make the changes and the outcomes you expect. The more transparent you are with your customers, the more understanding they'll be.

Marketer Neil Patel is a good example of this kind of transparency. For a number of years, he made a particular software available for free. Eventually, however, the costs became too high and he was forced to start charging for portions of the software.

He sent a letter to his customers, clearly explaining what was happening. He detailed his costs, making it clear that he simply didn't have the resources to continue making everything available for free. Then he laid out exactly what would happen moving forward.

You would be wise to follow Neil's example. Explain why changes are happening, when they will take effect, and how the changes will affect customers.

During times of global crisis, it is especially important to keep the focus on customers. People will remember the actions you take. If you seek to serve your customers, even at the expense of profit, you will build up a huge amount of goodwill.

For example, during the coronavirus crisis, many companies sacrificed financial gain for the sake of their customers:

- Many educational companies made their resources free to parents who were suddenly forced to homeschool their children.
- Audible gave away free audiobooks for kids.
- Moz provided free courses on search engine optimization to help businesses strengthen their online presence.
- Loom offered significant discounts on their video recording platform so people could stay in touch with family and friends.
- Bill.com made their platform available for free for 90 days to anyone affected by the coronavirus.

All of these companies are losing out on potential profit by giving these things away for free. But customers will remember the actions taken by these businesses and will be much more likely to support them in the future.

It's about building your brand by doing good for others, instead of focusing on the bottom line.

Bottom line: If you keep the focus on customers, there's a much greater chance that your business will weather the tough times.

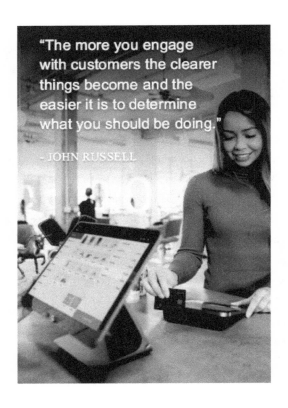

"The more you engage with customers the clearer things become and the easier it is to determine what you should be doing."

- JOHN RUSSELL

Conduct a SWOT Analysis

If you want to succeed as a small business owner, you must be willing to honestly evaluate how things are going. You can't ignore problems. You can't just hope that things get better. You must take a long and hard look at your business and then make changes based on what you see.

A SWOT (strengths, weaknesses, opportunities, threats) analysis provides you with a framework for analyzing your business. It helps you identify what is and isn't working, spot potential growth opportunities, and prepare for external threats.

Let's look at each aspect.

Strengths

These are the things you have control over and are working well in your business. Focus on and try to develop these areas further. For example:

- Effective sales team
- Proprietary technology
- Proven marketing strategy
- Powerful systems/processes
- Strong customer base

Weaknesses

These are the things that aren't working well in your business. Your goal is to change or eliminate these things so that they don't continue to damage your business.

For example:

- Ineffective marketing strategy
- High production costs
- Low profit margin
- Poor customer retention
- Ineffective internal processes

Opportunities

These are external factors that have the potential to benefit your business. The more you can capitalize on these opportunities, the more success you'll have.

For example:

- New technology
- Less competition
- Fewer taxes
- New markets
- Improved economic environment

Threats

These are external factors that could possibly hurt your business. Either avoid these things or adapt to them.

For example:

- Increased competition
- Changing customer preferences
- Worsening economic conditions (recession)
- New regulations
- Significant technological changes

Performing a SWOT analysis is hard work. It's essential to be honest about the current state of things and acknowledge areas where you're struggling. This clear-headed analysis will help you overcome your weaknesses, capitalize on your strengths, and take advantage of unique opportunities.

Create Objectives and A Plan

Once you've done a SWOT analysis, take what you've learned and put it into action. Determine the objectives you'll pursue and create a plan for achieving those objectives. This will give you the clarity you need to move forward.

Start with your strengths. How will you double down on the things you're already doing well? Does your sales team have a high close rate? Focus on getting more prospects to the team. Do you have a large email list? Work on converting them from readers to buyers.

Then look at your weaknesses. How can you change, minimize, or even eliminate these areas? Is your profit margin low? Create a plan for reducing production costs. Do you have trouble keeping customers? Develop a customer retention strategy.

Move on to opportunities. Is there a new market you can move into? Can you implement a new technology that will help you be more efficient? Determine the greatest opportunities for your business and the steps you'll take to capitalize on those opportunities.

Finish with threats. How will you avoid or adapt to those things that could hurt your business? Do you need to take steps to adjust to new customer preferences? Do you need to change your pricing strategy to keep up with the competition?

Remember to create both objectives *and* a plan for how you'll meet those objectives. It's not enough to say, "I want to increase my profit margin." You also need to determine the specific steps you'll take to make that happen.

Your objectives need to be:

- Measurable. You must be able to determine whether you've hit your objective.
- Achievable. Be realistic in your goal setting. Aim for things that you can actually achieve.

Timely. Set a specific date by which you'll meet your objectives. This will give you a sense of urgency.

Reduce Costs

If you want your business to survive and thrive during difficult times, you'll likely need to reduce your costs. However, be careful and precise as you do this. Cut costs too much and your business may have a hard time recovering. Cut costs too little and you won't free up enough cash to keep your business going.

Follow this process to reduce your costs:

Start by cutting discretionary costs. These are costs that aren't necessary to run your business. Business lunches is a good example of a discretionary cost.

Yes, it may be helpful to meet clients over lunch, but it's not necessary. You can meet them over coffee or in your office and save quite a bit.

Other discretionary costs include:

- Coffee/tea for the whole office
- The highest speed internet (switch to a lower speed)
- Magazine subscriptions
- Off-site events
- Advertising

Next, look at ways you can reduce costs but still achieve the same outcomes. For example:

- Can you reduce travel costs by using videoconferencing technology?
- Can you cut IT costs by using less expensive cloud software?
- Can you reduce utility costs by finding ways to use less water or electricity?
- Get creative when looking at these costs.

Next, consider your office space costs. Your landlord may be willing to lower your rent or even create a new lease for you. Explain the challenges you're facing and the possible outcomes if you don't make significant changes. If your landlord won't reduce your rent, consider moving to a less expensive building.

- If your business is small enough, you may want to think about running it out of your home, at least temporarily. This can significantly reduce insurance costs, taxes, utilities, and more.

Also take a close look at your supply chain. Some of your suppliers may be willing to give you discounts, especially if you've been a good customer and always paid on time.

- If your current suppliers don't offer discounts, explore alternatives. If a new supplier offers you a discount, you may be able to leverage that with your current suppliers.

At some point, you'll need to think about reducing staffing costs. This is hard for every business owner. No one wants to put someone out of a job or reduce someone's income.

- However, if you want your business to survive, you have to be willing to make these hard decisions. Cutting staffing costs today ensures that you'll still have a business in the future.

- Before you lay people off, look for ways you can reduce employee hours or compensation. Obviously, you'll need to communicate clearly with your employees. Explain why you're cutting these things and how long you expect these measures to last.

- If a reduction in hours or compensation isn't enough, you'll have to reduce your workforce.

"I attribute my success to this: I never gave or took any excuse."

- FLORENCE NIGHTINGALE

Cutting costs isn't a fun thing. You and your employees will have to make sacrifices. You'll have to give up perks and luxuries. But it's important to look at the big picture.

The actions you take today will produce results long into the future. Sacrificing in the present increases the chances of your business surviving for years to come.

Manage Your Cash Flow

Your cash flow is what will ultimately determine whether your business survives. Every month you have cash come into your business in the form of payments from customers or clients. You also have cash going out of your business for expenses like rent, supplies, and salaries.

Cash is King

Now, to be clear, when we say "cash", we don't necessarily mean actual cash. We simply mean money going into and out of your bank account.

Not having enough incoming cash is one of the biggest reasons small businesses go under. When you run out of cash, you can't pay your bills, purchase supplies, or any of the other necessary tasks to keep things running.

This means you need to pay very close attention to your cash flow.

Here's a quick way to evaluate your cash flow:

1. At the end of the month, add up your total sales.
2. Total all purchases that you still must pay for.
3. Calculate the difference.

For example, let's say you have $10,000 in sales. You still owe $6,000 for purchases. Your cash flow is approximately $4,000. If you have negative cash flow, you'll need to make up the difference in the next month. The more you fall behind, the harder it is to make up the difference.

If you have accounting software, you should be able to create a detailed cash flow report relatively easily.

If you find yourself struggling with cash flow, you do have some options, such as:

- You can sell assets to bring in additional cash. For example, you could sell a company vehicle or a piece of machinery.
- You can get a working capital line of credit. You are given a set amount of credit from which you can draw when cash

is tight and pay back when you have surplus cash. You only pay interest on what you borrow. For example, if you have a $10,000 line of credit and borrow $5,000, you only pay interest on the $5,000.

As much as possible, stay abreast of your cash flow. Send out invoices in a timely fashion and follow up with customers who fall behind on payments. Pay your own bills on time and try to plan accordingly for purchases.

Cash really is king.

Meet With An Accountant

Creativity is great - but not in accounting.

- CHARLES SCOTT

Prioritize meeting with an accountant

As you work to stabilize and strengthen your business, you would be wise to meet with a certified accountant. There are a number of reasons for this.

First, they can help you implement money-saving tax strategies. Taxes are complicated, especially when you're running a business. There are a number of specific actions you can take to reduce your tax burden.

For example, you can:

- Change the depreciation method used on your assets
- Defer income to the following year

- Restructure your business
- Maximize expense deductions

Because tax laws are so convoluted, many of these strategies are not intuitive. An accountant can help you know what actions to take.

Second, an accountant may be able to help you secure financial assistance from the local, state, or federal government.

Because small businesses are good for the economy, many government agencies are willing to provide financial aid for struggling businesses.

For example, the Small Business Association offers low interest loans and grants to qualifying businesses. Some state and city government organizations also have relief programs designed to strengthen small businesses. An accountant can help you find and secure government funding for your business.

Finally, an accountant can help you think through critical financial decisions.

Many business owners struggle to absorb all the financial details about their company. This is common and nothing to be ashamed of. However, if you struggle in this way, it can make it challenging to stay abreast of important numbers like cash flow.

An accountant can crunch all the numbers for you and then provide you with relatively easy-to-digest reports. They can also give you guidance as you make important decisions like what costs to cut.

Use Low-Cost Marketing

Marketing is a double-edged sword. On the one hand, it costs money to get your company name out there. Obviously, money you spend on marketing can't be spent on essential things like payroll and bills. On the other hand, if you stop doing marketing, you connect with fewer customers, which also decreases available funds.

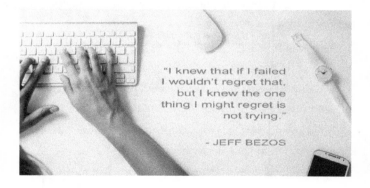

"I knew that if I failed I wouldn't regret that, but I knew the one thing I might regret is not trying."

- JEFF BEZOS

So, what should you do when your business is struggling? Should you cut your marketing budget? Should you double down on marketing?

Answer: yes.

Use low-cost marketing to simultaneously cut your budget and increase your efforts. Traditional advertising methods such as television, radio, and billboards tend to be pretty expensive.

You don't need to use these strategies to get in front of customers. Other techniques can be just as effective at a fraction of the cost.

For example:

- Regularly ask your existing clients for referrals. If you've provided your clients with great service, they'll be glad to send people your way.
- Local business networking groups are a great way to connect with potential clients in your community.
- Trade fairs or business meetups allow you to connect with key individuals in your industry.
- Write guest blog posts for websites in your industry.
- Appear on podcasts that your audience listens to.
- Develop strategic business partnerships that foster cross-promotion (you promote them, and they promote you).
- Build an email list and then consistently send out valuable information to your subscribers.
- Sponsor local events (charitable, sporting, and more).
- Maintain a consistent presence on various social media platforms.
- Create highly targeted online advertisements. This can be done for just a few dollars per day.
- Develop a cold calling strategy and make calls each day.
- Develop relationships with influencers who may be willing to promote your products.
- Create an affiliate program that rewards those who promote your products.

- Host events or classes (locally or online).
- Offer to speak at local business groups, community colleges, libraries, and conferences.
- Create a YouTube channel where you consistently deliver valuable information.
- Run online contests using a platform like Gleam.io or King Sumo.
- Offer a free trial of your product and create a process to turn those free trials into paying customers.
- Livestream from your workplace to show others what happens behind the scenes.

When it comes to marketing, you're only limited by your imagination.

Get creative and step outside your comfort zone. Reach out to people you normally would not.

Thanks to the internet and smartphones, marketing is easier and cheaper than ever. Take advantage of the connected world in which we live.

Be Persistent, Be Creative, and Pivot

What separates businesses that fail from those that thrive? Persistence and creativity. Successful businesses persist through challenging times and come up with creative solutions to difficult challenges. They don't give up in the face of adversity. Sometimes they even pivot to a completely different business model.

Polaroid is an example of a company that didn't approach problems with persistence or creativity. They failed to pivot when it really mattered.

As digital photography began to take over in the late 90's, Polaroid executives continued to insist that people wanted hard copy photos. They ignored the massive issue that was staring them in the face and wouldn't consider any other business model.

As a result, they were forced to file for bankruptcy in 2001. The once-great company was largely destroyed.

Yelp, on the other hand, used creativity and persistence to overcome difficulties. The service started as a platform for getting recommendations from friends. Even though they managed to get $1 million in funding, they couldn't seem to get much traction.

They noticed, however, that people enjoyed writing reviews of local businesses. They pivoted to focus on making it easy to write reviews and the rest is history.

Even in the worst circumstances, there are still options.

During the coronavirus pandemic of 2020, many companies pivoted in big ways:

- Anheuser-Busch began manufacturing hand sanitizer.
- Hanes started producing medical masks.
- Lyft used their huge fleet of cars to deliver medical supplies.
- Ford used its infrastructure to make ventilators and medical face shields.
- Farmers Restaurant Group shifted to delivering food supplies to customers.

How can you pivot in your business, so you stay afloat and meet the demand of your clients?

There are numerous ways you can pivot your business:

- Utilize new sales channels. If you run a brick-and-mortar business, consider also selling online.

- Segment your customers. 80% of your revenue comes from 20% of your customers. Instead of trying to please everyone, focus on the 20%.

- Focus on a feature. If you sell a product that has one particularly popular feature, focus much more heavily on that feature (like Yelp did with reviews).

- Change your revenue model. Historically, journalism relied heavily on subscriptions for funding. As we've moved into the internet era, many have pivoted to relying on advertising.

- Change your pricing and positioning. If you can't compete with someone on price, compete on quality, or vice versa.

- Adopt new technology. New tech can help you reach more customers. For example, if you're a tutoring company, using a platform like Zoom allows you to communicate with people virtually.

The reality is that every business faces challenges. Technology is constantly changing. The market is always in flux to some degree. New competitors regularly emerge.

These difficulties don't need to sink your business. Don't give up. Persistence produces success.

As Jim Collins said in *How The Mighty Fall:*

The path out of darkness begins with those exasperatingly persistent individuals who are constitutionally incapable of capitulation. It's one thing to suffer a staggering defeat – as will likely happen to every enduring business and social enterprise at some point in its history – and entirely another to give up on the values and aspirations that make the protracted struggle worthwhile. Failure is not so much a physical state as a state of mind; success is falling down, and getting up one more time, without end.

If you fall, get back up. Again, and again.

Take Action Today

If you want your business to survive the storms, you must take effective action immediately. Avoid just trying to wait it out, hoping things will get better. As is commonly said, hope is not a strategy.

It is the doers who are successful: those who confront the challenge head on, map out a strategy for change, and begin acting on that strategy.

We've talked about numerous steps that will strengthen your business:

- Manage your mindset.
- Clarify the problem.
- Focus on customers.
- Conduct a SWOT analysis.
- Create objectives and a plan.
- Reduce costs.
- Use low-cost marketing.
- Be persistent and creative.

Each of these steps requires work. You must be willing to dig into your business to figure out what isn't working. Create a clear plan of attack that you will diligently follow. You have to make hard decisions about what costs to cut and get creative with low-cost marketing.

If you take action on these things, you will dramatically increase the odds of your survival. You will tip the scales in your favor.

During the dark days of WWII, Winston Churchill famously urged the British people to, *"...never give in, never give in, never, never, never, never-in nothing, great or small, large or petty - never give in except to convictions of honor and good sense. Never yield to force; never yield to the apparently overwhelming might of the enemy."*

It was that never-say-die attitude that helped Britain stay afloat in the face of incredible difficulties.

The same attitude will keep your business afloat as well.

Resources the Author Recommends

CPSIA information can be obtained
at www.ICGtesting.com
Printed in the USA
LVHW091134080221
678694LV00004B/406